Day *and* Night

D1738661

Day *and* Night

by

Dorothy Livesay

OOLICHAN BOOKS
FERNIE, BRITISH COLUMBIA, CANADA
2011

Library and Archives Canada Cataloguing in Publication

Livesay, Dorothy, 1909-1996
    Day and night / Dorothy Livesay.

Poems.
Originally publ.: Toronto : Ryserson Press, 1944.

ISBN 978-0-88982-281-8

    I. Title.

PS8523.I82D3 2011   C811'.54   C2011-906431-6

We gratefully acknowledge the financial support of the Canada Council for the Arts, the British Columbia Arts Council through the BC Ministry of Tourism, Culture, and the Arts, and the Government of Canada through the Book Publishing Industry Development Program, for our publishing activities.

Published by
Oolichan Books
P.O. Box 2278
Fernie, British Columbia
Canada V0B 1M0

www.oolichan.com

Printed in Canada.

MIX
Paper from
responsible sources
FSC
www.fsc.org   FSC® C013916

FOREWARD

Welcome to this new publication of Dorothy Livesay's *Day and Night*. We have endeavoured to create a book that is sympathetic to the original Ryerson Press edition both in style and feel. The intent is to return Livesay's work to the public in a form close to which it was originally envisioned.

Day and Night represents Livesay's transition from her life in Central Canada to creating a new life for herself and her family on the West Coast. Poems from both phases are included here as she firmly established herself as an activist and poet.

While the poems of *Day and Night* speak to life during the Great Depression and the Second World War, they often feel strikingly contemporary. The issues with which Livesay grappled remain with us today and the messages she articulated are ones we well might heed.

Special thanks are due to the office of the Poet Laureate of Vancouver for the vision of celebrating the literary history of the Vancouver and to the City of Vancouver and the Association of Book Publishers of B.C. for supporting this vision. The support of these organizations made this work possible.

ACKNOWLEDGEMENT
(FROM THE 1944 EDITION)

Most of these poems have been printed in: *Poetry* (Chicago), *The Canadian Forum*, *The Canadian Poetry Magazine*, *New Frontier*, *Contemporary Verse*, *Canadian Review of Music and Art*, and *First Statement*.

To
ALAN AND JEAN CRAWLEY
(gardeners)

Contents

DAY *and* NIGHT

SEVEN POEMS

I

A SHELL burst in my mind
Upheaving roots since birth, perhaps, confined
Before I dreamed
The devastation there outlined.

And so my body now
Owes no allegiance to the scythe and plough:
I, dispossessed
Count no blossoms on the bough.

I build on no man's land
A city not my own, with others planned
By others dreamed,
And with a new race forged and manned!

II

From the husk of the old world
To the new I fly
Strong wings beating
In a bluer sky

Where old men stretch not
Their vampire necks
And young men vaunt not
Their sunburnt backs

Where jewelled women
With glittering breasts
Suck not the life-blood
From young nests

But where the cradled
Infant rocks
While cloudy sheep
Caress his locks

And where the golden
Apples blow
In easy bliss
Upon a bough.

Seven Poems

III

Out of the turmoil mustered up by day
We may not free our hands, nor turn our heads to pray–
So tight the knot our sunlight ties.

So firm the hold of voices, thoughts are drowned
The river's chant is lost, in splintering gunshot sound:
Or from its song the essence dies.

Brightness was all, when earth lay primitive
Fair to the hands' fresh touch, ready to burst and live:
Now in her womb corrosion lies.

Therefore we search alone the shuttered dark
Where faces of the dead shine luminous, a spark
Of lightning from encircled skies:

Therefore we seek the peace of broken ground
After the wars have buried all the young, and found
Dark remedy for shining eyes . . .

Therefore we hide our faces; make no sound.

IV

On a night like this, the Ides of March perhaps,
Spring will arrest your muscles and a raid
Of hands will light on you, and cry out: "Choose."
Incisive fingers on your shoulder-blade,
Open sockets for stampeding news.

"Listen child." And you know the answer held
You face the pitiless eyes and open wide
Your own, like shock observers; as they say
The words no fluttering flag of fear could hide:
"The operation failed. He died today."

And if the words were different: "War's declared."
There is no difference, the thought is one.
This the expected shock, the Judas-kiss
A flower cup uncurling into sun
Childhood's leaves warned by the dark of this.

We grew, and munitions matched us, laboratories
Weighed the ingredients; magnifying glass
Revealed death's desert in a finger-nail
Of dust. Whatever door we ought to pass
Was marked with chalk. All sesames would fail.

This is not news, but a resolution passed
After hard labor, bitterness of sides.
Tenseness relaxed, you knew it all your days:
There would be one man missing, one who hides
His cunning hand from thunder with the "nays."

Seven Poems

Impartially the chairman-undertaker
Smiling casts his vote, announces death
Speculates on population where
Our wombs are lacerated, lovers' breath
Is torn asunder in the cool March air.

We are the children long prepared for dust
Ready in bone, the wrist a pulsing pain;
On a precarious railway-rib we lie
Our limbs long ready for the armored train—
Ears to the ground and bare eyes to the sky.

V

The fallow mind in winter knows, its scope
And wide horizon are made narrow by
The rim of early dusk, descending blinds—
Last summer's rocket buried under sand.
To soar and spin, to take the hand and whip
A leash of fiery comets through the sky:
To be crier or prophet, John or Isaiah, these
Wait in the mind for the world's turning phase:
The time she lifts her head from blood-soaked fields,
From one-eyed houses, shattered, gaping towns,
The time she sees her brother sun, and bares
Her ribs to his remembered healing blaze—
Then will the mind take a new stature on
And children thrive, who late last year were bombed.

Seven Poems

VI

The child looks out from doors too high and wide for him
On words spun large as suns, huge meanings sprayed on
    tree
And roadway, spreading fields, not to be caught and
    clapped
Together in a rosy nave, the sun no coin
For fingers to indent.   The child runs out to stare
At masterful young men who bat at a tennis ball
At giants in kilt skirts whose march is purposeful
At mothers in cool gowns who move about like moons
Upon the eternal lawns, low laughter shimmering
About their curving mouths.

             The child leans on the future,
Slender tree ungainly rooted there by private worlds
Who knew a private ecstasy unshared by him
But let the memory slip and reared a hedge
Of bristling phrases, last year's bills, and week-ends
    snatched
In secret hate; his room laid waste when radios
Are tuned, when rumor's blatant voice hits nerve,
Dries tissue, brittles down
The new unmolded bone.   The child in cities toddling up
A stifling reach of stair, gains window-seat:
How consternation puckers up his eyes—at space
Unplanted, seed unwanted, wars unwarranted
Consuming his small, thankless growing place!

VII

And life goes on. And here
We hold a leaf upon the eyes
And its green ribs press down like veins
Into the nerve and sinew of ourselves.
Your finger-tip on eyelid, or my brows
Bent in the conclave of your cheek,
Spurs vibrant nerve to life, adheres like leaf to stem
Stem into tree, tree rooted into earth.

No hazard here, for we
Like sleepers plunging deep
Into recurring waves of dream
Cannot awake from that connected bliss.
We are asleep on the long limb of time.

1934-1940.

THE OUTRIDER

"Swift outrider of lumbering earth."

—C. DAY LEWIS

For Raymond Knister

PROLOGUE

HE WHO was alien has retraced the road
Unleashed, returns to this familiar earth.
The gate falls open at his touch, the house
Receives him without wonder, as an elm
Accepts her brood of birds. Along his road
Crows' charivari chattering announce
His coming to each thronging sentry-post.

The old man standing with his hayfork high
Can let it rest, mid-air, and burden fails
And falls within the sun-dipped gloom of barn.
The young boy bowed behind the clicking mow
Feels his spine stiffen as if birds had whirred
Behind him, or a storm had clapped its clouds.
A girl, chin pressed upon a broom, will stir
As a warm wave of wonder sweeps her out
Whither her musings never leapt before.
And so it is.

His coming dreamed of long
In the recesses of thinking, in the hard
Hills climbed, his face a resting-place.
In winter warming hands at roaring stove
His doings slumbering as autumn wood . . .
And so it is. Now summer's all swept clean
He comes with eyes more piercing than before
And scrapes his boots—swinging wide the door.

19

The Outrider

I

The year we came, it was all stone picking:
Sun on your fiery back, and the earth
Grimly hanging on to her own. And the farm's end
A cedar bog to clear. But in the dry season
Not enough drink for the cattle.
The children gathered blueberries, and ate corn meal.
We danced no festivals.

Children stretched lean to manhood. One day
Wind prying round, wrenched free the barn
And lightning had the whole hay crop
Flaming to heaven. Trying to save the horse
Arthur was stifled. His black bones
We buried under the elm.

I stumble around now, trying to see it clearly.
Incessantly driven to feed our own ones, but friendly
     to neighbors:
Not like the crows, hungry for goslings,
But sober, sitting down Sunday for rest-time
Contented with laughter.

I stumble around now, lame old farm dog:
When I'm gone, one less hunger
And the hay still to be mown.

.   .   .   .   .

The Outrider

The buggy on that whirling autumn day
Swayed in a rain rut, nearly overturned.
And you stood by the roadside, brown and gay,
Black hair drawn tight in pigtails and your eyes
Searching the sky. Brave was your body then
And I brought you home to discover the answer to
    hunger.
The peace of loving, the stay to restlessness.

Trembling as a birch tree to a boy's swinging
You were again and again my own small love.
But love was never enough, though children sprang
Year after year from your loins—never enough
For my yearning though your eyes burned strangely—
And earth has kept you far more fierce and safe.

     . . . . .

My mother caught me in her skirts and tossed me high
    High into hay I bounced.
The straw tickled and a swallow, frightened, flew
    Before my heart could cry.

I remember this, the startling day of early fear,
    Bird beating me back
And somehow, no way—hard to know why or where
    she was no longer near.

Brothers would later tease me with a feather tail
    or loose a crow they caught
And I must swallow the fear with my hunger, to learn
    how the yearned for will fail

The Outrider

How the expected sunlight will shrivel your pounding heart,
    the seed you plant be killed
The apple be bitter with worm, but your honesty firm
    seeking another start.

      ·   ·   ·   ·

I grew up one evening , much alone—
Resolved to plunge. The thing I feared, the crow,
Was hoarse with calling, whirling, diving down
And suddenly his urgent social bent
Was answer to my inwardness. His cry
Throbbed and echoed in my head, his wings
Caught all reflections in my mirrored mind.
I would then follow where his footless tread
Led on; I would no longer be the beast
Who ploughed a straight line to the barrier
And swung back on his steps—my father's son.
It would take long. But from that summer on
My heart was set. I raced through swinging air,
Rumpled my head with laughter in the clouds.

The Outrider

II

It was different, different
From the thoughts I had.
Asphalt and factory walls are not
Soft ending to the road.

It was different, different
Standing tight in line
Forgetting buffeting clouds above
Trying to look a man.

It was different, different
To lift the lever arm
And see the farm beasts revolving by
Their dripping blood still warm.

On lazier afternoons
Deep in clover scent
Neither beast nor I could dream
What the speed-up meant.

A thousand men go home
And I a thousandth part
Wedged in a work more sinister
That hitching horse and cart.

Dark because you're beaten
By a boss's mind:
A single move uneven turned
Will set you in the wind.

The Outrider

His mercy is a calculation
Worse than a hurricane—
Weather you can grumble at
But men can make you groan.

      .   .   .   .   .

        (Down in the washroom
           leaflets are passed.
        "Say, Joe, you sure
           got those out fast."

        "Yes. Now's the time
           to give them the gate:
        Speed-up right here
           is legitimate!"

        An older worker stares:
           his wizened face
        Sceptical still—
           Years in the trace.

        But young, lean face
           opposite me
        Reads, and alert
           watches to see

        Who will respond
           who's first to talk—
        Our eyes meet, and greet
           as a key fits the lock.)

The Outrider

Early morning
stirs the street
men go by
on urgent feet.

Early morning
litter still
in the gutters
on the sill.

Early morning
sky shows blue
men are marching
two and two.

Men are surging
past the gate
where last week no one
dared be late:

Surging—though
a siren's shrieks
warn that someone
called the dicks . . .

. . . . . .

It was different, different
Because I learned: for this
You plough the fields and scatter
The toil of days and years.

The Outrider

You die in harness and are proud ,
Of earthen servitude
While others that live in chains have sought
To shake the rotting wood

Upheave the very earth, if need
Insist, banish the fence
Between a neighbor's grudging hate
Rise in our own defence

Against the smooth-tongued salesman
"The cottage built for two"
The haggling on market days
Desperate to know

How winter's service shall be slaved—
Will this hay last the year—
Where are the taxes coming from—
Must we sell the mare?

Cities that sell their toil, must put
Possessiveness to shame
And draw you to them in the fight:
The battle is the same

The blowing silver barley grain
And skyline wide, serene—
These shall be your gift to those
Who wield the world's machine!

The Outrider

III

This is your signpost: follow your hands, and dig.
After, the many will have parachutes
For air delight. Not veering with the crow
But throbbing, conscious, knowing where to go.
There's time for flying. Dig up crumbling roots,
Eradicate the underbrush and twig—
Pull snapping thistle out and stubborn sloe—
Those backward ramblers who insist they know.

Employ your summertime, at union rate:
Conveying energy on this green belt
Of earth assembled, swiftly known and felt.
Faster! Speed-up is here legitimate:
Employ your summertime, before the thrust
Of winter wind would harden down the dust.

The Outrider

We prayed for miracles: the prairie dry,
Our bread became a blister in the sun;
We watched the serene untouchable vault of sky
—In vain our bitter labor had been done.

We prayed to see the racing clouds at bay
Rumpled like sheets after a night of joy,
To stand quite still and let the deluged day
Of rain's releasing, surge up and destroy.

We prayed for miracles, and had no wands
Nor wits about us; strained in a pointed prayer
We were so many windmills without hands
To whirl and drag the water up to air.

A runner sent ahead, returned with news:
"There is no milk nor honey flowing there.
Others allay the thirst with their own blood
Cool with their sweat, and fertilize despair."

O new found land! Sudden release of lungs,
Our own breath blows the world! Our veins, unbound
Set free the fighting heart. We speak with tongues—
This struggle is our miracle new found.

1935.

DAY AND NIGHT

I

DAWN, red and angry, whistled loud and sends
A geysered shaft of steam searching the air.
Scream after scream announces that the churn
Of life must move, the giant arm command.
Men in a steam, a moving human belt
Move into sockets, every one a bolt.
The fun begins, a humming whirring drum—
Men do a dance in time to the machines.

One step forward
Two steps back
Shove the lever,
Push it back

While Arnot whirls
A roundabout
And Geoghan shuffles
Bolts about

One step forward
Hear it crack
Smashing rhythm—
Two steps back

Your heart-beat pounds
Against your throat
The roaring voices
Drown your shout

Day and Night

Across the way
A writhing whack
Sets you spinning
Two steps back—

One step forward
Two steps back.

Day and Night

II

Day and night are rising and falling
Night and day shift gears and slip rattling
Down the runway, shot into storerooms
Where only arms and a note-book remember
The record of evil, the sum of commitments.
We move as through sleep's revolving memories
Piling up hatred, stealing the remnants
Doors forever folding before us—
And where is the recompense, on what agenda
Will you set love down? Who knows of peace?

Day and night
Night and day
Light rips into ribbons
What we say

I called to love
Deep in dream:
Be with me in the daylight
As in gloom.

Be with me in the pounding
In the knives against my back
Set your voice resounding
Above the steel's whip crack

Day and Night

High and sweet
Sweet and high
Hold, hold up the sunlight
In the sky!
Day and night
Night and day
Tear up all the silence
Find the words I could not say . . .

Day and Night

III

We were stoking coal in the furnaces; red hot
They gleamed, burning our skins away, his and mine.
We were working together, night and day, and knew
Each other's stroke; and without words exchanged
And understanding about kids at home,
The landlord's jaw, wage-cuts and overtime.

We were like buddies, see? Until they said
That nigger is too smart the way he smiles
And sauces back the foreman; he might say
Too much one day, to others changing shifts.
Therefore they cut him down, who flowered at night
And raised me up, day hanging over night—
So furnaces could still consume our withered skin.

Shadrach, Mechak and Abednego
Turn in the furnace, whirling slow.

> Lord, I'm burnin' in the fire
> Lord, I'm steppin' on the coal
> Lord, I'm blacker than my brother
> Blow your breath down here.

> Boss, I'm smothered in the darkness
> Boss, I'm shrivellin' in the flames
> Boss, I'm blacker than my brother
> Blow your breath down here.

Shadrach, Mechak and Abednego
Burn in the furnace, whirling slow.

Day and Night

IV

Up in the roller room, men swing steel
Swing it, zoom; and cut it, crash.
Up in the dark the welder's torch
Makes sparks fly like lightning's reel.

Now I remember storm on a field
The trees bow tense before the blow
Even the jittering sparrow's talk
Ripples in the still tree shield.

We are in storm that has no cease
No lull before, no after time
When green with rain the grasses grow
And air is sweet with fresh increase.

We bear the burden home to bed
The furnace glows within our hearts:
Our bodies hammered through the night
Are welded into bitter bread.

Bitter, yes:
But listen, friend
We are mightier
In the end

We have ears
Alert to seize
A weakness
In the foreman's ease

Day and Night

We have eyes
To look across
The bosses' profit
At our loss.

Are you waiting?
Wait with us
After evening
There's a hush

Use it not
For love's slow count:
Add up hate
And let it mount

The wheels may whirr
A roundabout
And neighbor's shuffle
Drown your shout

The wheel must limp
Till it hangs still
And crumpled men
Pour down the hill.

Day and night
Night and day—
Till life is turned
The other way!

1935.

LORCA

For Federico Garcia Lorca, Spanish poet, shot by
Franco's men

WHEN veins congeal
And gesture is confounded
When pucker frowns no more
And voice's door
Is shut forever

On such a night
My bed will shrink
To single size
Sheets go cold
The heart hammer
With life-loud clamor
While someone covers up the eyes.

Ears are given
To hear the silence driven in
Nailed down.
And we descend now down from heaven
Into earth's mold, down.

While you—
You hold the light
Unbroken.

When you lived
Day shone from your face:
Now the sun rays search
And find no answering torch.

Lorca

If you were living now
This cliffside tree
And its embracing bough
Would speak to me.

If you were speaking now
The waves below
Would be the organ stops
For breath to blow.

And if your rigid head
Flung back its hair
Gulls in a sickle flight
Would circle there.

> *You make the flight*
> *Unbroken*

You are alive!
O grass flash emerald sight
Dash of dog for ball
And skipping rope's bright blink
Lashing the light!

High in cloud
The sunset fruits are basketed
And fountains curl their plumes
On statue stone.
In secret thicket mold
Lovers defend their hold,
Old couples hearing whisperings
Touch in a handclasp, quivering.

Lorca

For you sang out aloud
Arching the silent wood
To stretch itself, tiptoe,
Above the crowd . . .

> *You hold the word*
> *Unspoken*

You breathe. You be.
Bare, stripped light
Time's fragment flagged
Against the dark.

You dance. Explode
Unchallenged through the door
As bullets burst
Long deaths ago, your breast.

And song outsoars
The bomber's range
Serene with wind—
Manoeuvred cloud.

> *Light flight and word*
> *The unassailed, the token!*

1939.

PRELUDE FOR SPRING

THESE dreams abound:
Foot's leap to shore
Above the sound
Of river's roar—
Disabled door
Banged and barricaded.
Then on, on
Furrow, fawn
Through wall and wood
So fast no daring could
Tear off the hood
Unmask the soul pursued.

Slash underbrush
Tear bough and branch
Seek cover, rabbits' burrow—
Hush!

He comes. Insistent, sure
Proud prowler, this pursuer comes
Noiseless, no wind-stir
No leaf-turn over;
Together quiet creeps on twig,
Hush hovers in his hands.

How loud heart's thump—
Persistent pump
Sucks down, down sap
Then up in surge
(Axe striking stump).

Prelude for Spring

How breezy breath—
Too strong a wind
Scatters a stir
Where feathers are.
Bustles a bough.

How blind two eyes
Shuttling to-fro
Not weaving light
Nor sight . . .
In darkness flow.

(Only the self is loud;
World's whisperless.)

Dive down then, scuttle under:
Run, fearless of feet's thunder.
Somehow, the road rolls back in mist
Here is the meadow where we kissed
And here the horses, galloping
We rode upon in spring . . .

O beat of air, wing beat
Scatter of rain, sleet,
Resisting leaves,
Retarding feet

And drip of rain, leaf drip
Sting on cheek and lip
Tearing pores
With lash of whip

Prelude for Spring

And hoof's away, heart's hoof
Down greening lanes, with roof
Of cherry blow
And apple puff—

O green wet, sun lit
Soaked earth's glitter!
Down mouth, to munch
Up hoof, to canter

Through willow lanes
A gold-shaft shower,
Embracing elms
That lack leaf-lustre

And copse' cool bed
All lavendered
With scentless, sweet
Hepatica—

Till side by side
In fields' brown furrow
Swathe sunlight over
Every shadow!

But still
On heart's high hill
And summit of
A day's delight

Prelude for Spring

Still will he swoop
From heaven's height
Soaring unspent,
Still will he stoop to brush
Wing tip on hair,
Fan mind with fear.

And now the chill
Raw sun
Goes greener still—
The sky
Cracks like an icicle:

Frozen, foot-locked
Heart choked and chafed
Wing-battered and unsafe,
Grovel to ground!
A cry
Lashes the sky—

These dreams abound.

1939.

SERENADE FOR STRINGS

For Peter

I

At nine from behind the door
The tap tapping
Is furtive, insistent:
Recurrent, imperative
The I AM crying
Exhorting, compelling.

At eleven louder!
Wilderness shaking
Boulders uprolling
Mountain creating

And deep in the cavern
No longer the hammer
Faintly insistent
No longer the pickaxe
Desperate to save us
But minute by minute
The terrible knocking
God at the threshold!
Knocking down darkness
Battering daylight.

II

O green field
O sun soaked
On lavish emerald
Blade and sharp bud piercing
O green field
Cover and possess me
Shield me in brightness now
From the knocking
The terrible knocking . . . .

Serenade for Strings

III

Again . . . Again . . . O again.
Midnight. A new day.
Day of days
Night of nights
Lord of lords.

Good Lord deliver us
Deliver us of the new lord
Too proud for prison
Too urgent for the grave . . .
Deliver us, deliver us.

> *O God the knocking*
> *The knocking attacking*
> *No breath to fight it*
> *No thought to bridge it*
> *Bare body wracked and writhing*
> *Hammered and hollowed*
> *To airless heaving.*

IV

The clock now. Morning.
Morning come creeping
Scrublady slishing
And sloshing the waxway
And crying O world
Come clean
Clean for the newborn
The sun soon rising . . .

Rising and soaring
On into high gear . . .
Sudden knowledge!
Easy speedway
Open country
Hills low-flying
Birds up brooding
Clouds caressing
A burning noon-day . . .

Now double wing-beat
Breasting body
Till cloudways open
Heaven trembles:
   And blinding
      searing
         terrifying
            cry!

The final bolt has fallen.
The firmament is riven.

Serenade for Strings

V

Now it is done.
Relax. Release.
And here, behold your handiwork:
Behold—a man!

1941.

FIVE POEMS

For Marcia

I

IN the dream was no kiss
No banners were upshaken
The sure, unsevered bonds of bliss
Were the hands untaken

In the dream no faltering
Grew between your tree and mine
Wind silenced us and sun embraced
We seized no outward sign

In the dream all burden fell
Sheer away; bare breathing left—
Bare eyes and light-cleft minds were formed
And found, never to be bereft.

It was the dream I saw again
Meeting your person in the room
The dream, electrified; since, I am free:
Bird funneling night flight alone.

II

Your face is new; strange;
Yet infinitely known
Loved in some century
Grass swept, tree sown.

I memorize
The lineaments, so lean
Steel bird prey intent
Flight imminent

I see your stride (no walk)
Cleaving the air,
Cloud treading, your hair
Sickle bent.

O early, early
Before dawn whispers
Before day fingers
The faulty doorway

Early in the late
Moon-tossed night
Your face a flash
Foreruns the light.

III

Early I lifted the oars of day
Sped over silent water
Early the wings of gulls found shadow
Sky's face flashing, mirrored.

Early morning is heart alone
No man shouting, no one
No planes soaring, death destroying
No shattered street a ruin.

Early is barely reachable
Soars beyond our knowing:
We are late sleepers, drugged in dark
Aliens all, to morning . . .

Five Poems

IV

Night's soft armor welds me into thought
Pliant and engaging; warm dark,
No scintillations to distract
Nor any restless ray, moon-shot.
I am still of all but breathing—
No throbbing eye, no pulse; and a hushed heart.

. . . . . .

Sometimes at rest, the bones assume
World's weight, hold us dumb
We cannot lift a finger, flick
An eyelash, wag a tongue:
Breath is the only fluctuation in
Death's posture, stoney, dumb.

Then is all sound fled
Flown from the fluted ear
Wind in the heavy head
Can find no corridor

And then is sight so bound
Lids petrified to earth
Only one light is found—
Imagination's going forth!

Only the heaven sent
Pulse of the universe
Beats through the buried heart
Its steady course.

Five Poems

V

Your words beat out in space—
Distant drums under the hum of day
Only the hunter hurries for
Only the parched heart hears.

Look, it takes long to grow a listener
To bend his bough, let fall his leaf to earth;
Upward and on his own words speeding
Leaps the self to light.

But wind is teacher. Rain is kind
Down-sailing, soaking deep
And summer ruddying to sear
Reiterates the drift:

Be earthward bound; and here
In the strata of flown flowers
And skeleton of leaf, set self down
Hurry ear to ground.

Not burials; not dust and ashes' crumbs
But world's own cry resounding!
The spacious, the distant, army of your answer
The fast approaching drums.

1942.

FANTASIA

For Helena Coleman

AND I have learned how diving's done
How breathing air, cool wafted trees
Clouds massed above the man-made tower
How these
Can live no more in eye and ear:
And mind be dumb
To all save Undine and her comb.

Imagination's underworld! where child goes down
Light as a feather. Water pressure
Hardly holds him, diving's easy
As the flight of bird in air
Or bomber drumming in his lair.

Child goes down, and laughingly
(He's not wanted yet, you see)
Catches fishes in his hand
Burrows toe in sifting sand
Seizes all the weeds about
To make a small sub-rosa boat

The up he bobs, as easily
As any blown balloon
To greet the bosky, brooding sky
And hunger for the sun.

                    .   .   .   .   .

Fantasia

And child grown taller, clothed in man's
Long limbs, and shaggy hair, his chin outthrust
Searches for years the rounded world
Climbs to its peaks, falls to its valleys green
Striding the trim and trailing towns
Fingering the fond arteries
Possessing things, and casting them
Cloakwise to earth for sleeping time . . .

Sometime the lust wanderer
Will sleep, will pause; will dream of plunging deep
Below it all, where he will need
No clock companion, thorn in flesh, no contact man
To urge him from the ground.
For flying's easy, if you do it diving
And diving is the self unmoored
Ranging and roving—man alone.

                    .   .   .   .   .

And I have learned how diving's done
Wherefore the many, many
Chose the watery stair
Down, down Virginia
With your fêted hair
Following after Shelley
Or woodcarvers I knew
(Bouchette; and Raymond, you)—
Here is the fascination
Of the salty stare:
And death is here.
Death courteous and calm, glass-smooth
His argument so suave, so water-worn
A weighted stone.

Fantasia

And death's deliberation, his
Most certain waiting-room
His patience with the patient, who will be
His for infinity . . .

So no astounded peerers
On the surface craft
No dragging nets, no cranes
No gnarled and toughened rope
Not any prayer nor pulley man-devised
Will shake the undersea
Or be
More than a brief torpedo, children's arrow
More than a gaudy top outspun
Its schedule done . . .

.   .   .   .   .

Wise to have learned: how diving's done
How breathing air, cool wafted trees
Clouds massed above the man-made tower
How these
Can live no more in eye and ear:
And mind be dumb
To all save Undine and her comb . . .

1942.

WEST COAST

PRELUDE

THIS hour: and we have seen a shabby town change face
And sandy soil be ripped of evergreen
And broom, born yellow into golden May
Scrapped farther up Grouse Mountain. We, who lay
In roses and green shade under the cherry tree
We too were rooted up, set loose to beg
Or borrow a new roof, accept a poorer view.
The tide had turned. That early gull adrift
On empty inlet, keel to sun, he was outrun
By humming plane, the flying boat on trial;
And pleasure schooner skirting the dark shore
Was soon nosed into harbor; for the grey gaunt giants,
Hunters of the skyline, convoy cruisers, they
Jostled the bay.

              We saw the shoreline ripped
And boxes set in tidy rows, a habitation for
A thousand children swept from farm and mine
Drawn to the hungry suction of the sea;
And saw the sunny slip where ferries sauntered in
Easing their stragglers into a sleepy street
Suddenly ablaze! And walls reared up, ship high,
Grim curtain for machine-gun rat-tat-tat
As caulkers set to work and welders steered
The starry shrapnel on a new laid keel.

West Coast

Where two or three had come, travellers to be met
Or mountain hikers holidaying high,
Now in a herd of thundering hard heels
Men surged for shop and ways, ten thousand strong
And bent for business, eager to belong.

High on our hill we watched, and saw
Morning become high noon, and the tide full.

West Coast

He who knew heaven is coming down the mountain
Is stirred with wonder; curious, even he—
Who sat with Horace at Soracte's heels
Lulled to the murmur of Virgillian bees,
Who bent eyes bookward in his earliest days
Sucking sunlight from a world of words
Dreaming to be word-welder, builder of these.
Till rain swept on him lacerating lines
Of woeful time; till sunlight burned hot steel
Into his shapeless heart, stoning it down
To hard defending, harder thought—
Then up, and words away, and books stamped under
Up to the gravelled trail, the crags far yonder
Feet firm on promontory, cloud encircled:
Where sun and rain blazed bliss on him
Night chasing day on snow-split mountain rim.

He who knew heaven stands among us, watching
His hand unfitted to this hammer-hold,
His heart not conscious of the anvil beat,
No visor for his eyes. Now he
Makes ships? For carrying love in hold,
Ah yes, for salting down old wisdom into kegs
For other hands to welcome—yes and yes!
But ships for men to fight upon
Ships to right the wrong upon?—
He hardly knows; he hesitates.

West Coast

And all about men flatten out the steel
With hammer beat, beat hammer, hammer beat
Shape it with sweat and muscle, shaped to fit
The nuzzle of a ship, a new sea-bird.
And all about the masked men strike the torch
Shaping the sides of ships with plate on plate
Riveting bolts with sea-resistent spark.
The hum, the drive of it!
The roar, the strive of it!
Each single soul to his own labor bent
Yet welded to his neighbor, for the toil
Fits all together in an endless chart,
The pattern-makers moving on
From ship to ship, galley to hold,
Until a new keel's laid, another scaffolding,
Till fire and sweat, muscle and oath and jest
Mingle to launch her down the vaulted ways—
A pearl-grey daughter leashed against the quays.

And why? What heaven-sent wanderer
Can see the ant-hill swarm and be at ease
Carrying his load of tools or wheeling truck
Slinging steel rods onto a derrick train?

He watched a day or so; waited his time
Stood in blacksmith's doorway where the furnaces
Bellied and glared, vomiting molten steel
Till the great moulder caught and shouldered it
Machine's male hands on feminine soft flesh
Creating features, fittings for a bride
A child of ocean still at berth, unscarred.

West Coast

Challenged, mind moved, but not to the blood warmed
Excitement seething in nerve's crevices
The ship, he saw, a symbol of conception
A giant scheme rearing to sky fruition:
But yet he stood without, a stranger still,
One hesitant to knock.

West Coast

II

So morning found him, morning's gossamer
Pearling the water, silvering the ships.
On morning shift, when sky and water melt
When men and women pour, with swinging pails
From ferry slip,
Pass through the gates, are billeted
And move, alert, toward the long grey shape
To find their home, their roof:
On morning shift, song burst from below the decks.
He bent his head, and heard, true as a bell
Andalusion love song; high amidships
Rumble of the rumba; in the hold
A youngster jived; and girls at hand
Trousered and kerchiefed, busy hammering
Whistled clear to call the Coolins.
Song! Song from the throat of morning bursting
High above rivet, chipper, torch—
Song from the heart of man at labor
Welding his words into the ship's side.

West Coast

FIRST VOICE:

Who have through mountain wall
Tunneled to dank pits
Where gas reeks, where weak light is life;
Who have on mountain side
Meagre as table bare, taken a wife
Made children, reared a roof;

Who fought in strikes and met starvation
Then back to pits again to face damnation
The dust sticking to throat, the cough, collapse
Then from the Sanitarium, down to sea
The sea-coast air, and ships a-building there:
Who breathe now, who find voice
And sing with the throat bare.

SECOND VOICE:

Who have through hail and storm, through endless rain
Cherished the crop, husbanded our flock.
Have builded fences, reared high dykes
Shifted the barn to upper ground
And with the hay half harvested, seen cloud
Crouch low again to pelt destruction down:
Seen trees and fences, horses, calves and lambs
Float helpless by, moaning their last faint cry—
Who from despair and loss returned to city's arms
And at the sea gate found a silver ship.

West Coast

THIRD VOICE:

Who have loved water, yearned for flood
Watched woolly clouds puffed from the piping sky
Who held the crumbling firmament in hand
And knew no seeds could breathe, no green life flow;
Who on the burnt spring grass cherished a crocus bloom
Until we cursed it, for it bore no bread.

Who had no walls, no home
No animals in barn
Only the rusted implements
Only the thistle, self-sown.

Who trekked bare-footed, underclothed
Greedy for fruit in Okanagan fields,
Thirsty for ocean even if salt it be:
Who have paused here, on brink of life again,
Build ships on quays, and bless the autumn rain.

FOURTH VOICE:

Who have been reared on rations and soup-kitchens
And sent from school unlearned, clutching at work
Out from the curling east to streaming west
Riding the rods with hobos, drug fiends, college students
And sleeping, at the country's end in flophouse—
A friend to jail, on easy terms with hunger.

West Coast

Who have lain low, known thin girls in an alley
Kissed under a bridge and pillowed on stone
Who raised a fist to a window, blind with anger
And demonstrated hate in the streets of the sleek:

Who have been thrown a bone and yapped at thrower
Who looked this gift horse sharply in the mouth
Who work, watching; who launch ships, wary
Waiting the year's turn, living to see . . .

We too are here, bent over bench and caulker
Our hearts awake; for now, our voices free:

West Coast

III

He who with Horace at Soracte's heels
Sat to the murmur of Virgillian bees:
He who knew heaven saw the gateway open
Heard the morning singing from the hold.
He who knew heaven seized on rivet, hammer
Ran to new keel laid on ways, to new life set
Ready for use, ready to break or build.
He who knew heaven found in men a singing
Lifted his heart and welded his own song:

> O man drift of the world
> This ferry is your fold
> Bearing you on to build
> Love in a ship's hold.

> Sprung from each land at war
> Squeezed through the open door
> Chinese boys who pour
> Sunflower seeds on floor

> Hungarians and Greeks
> Sicilian lad who speaks
> The softest tongue; and flicks
> Eyes at the laughing Czechs—

> And Paris French is heard
> Shot with the English word
> Watching a plumed white bird
> Whirl seaward.

West Coast

And German speaks, and Pole
And Ireland's growl
Each on his own assembly line
Attentive to his soul—

On man drift of the world
Here at the port unfurled
Each banner; and each song
Blooms from a ship's hold!

West Coast

FINALE

High on our hill we watched, and saw
Morning become high noon, and the tide full.
Saw children chequered on the western beach
And ferry boats plough back and forth, knocking the nose
Of tugboats, barges, freighters, convoys, cruisers
The harbor a great world of moving men
Geared to their own salvation, taking heart.
We watched gold sun wheel past the sombre park
Slip beyond Lion's Gate, illuminate
Cool purple skyline of the Island hills.
And to the hulls and houses silence came
Blinds down on tired eyes
Dark drew its blanket over trees and streets
Grey granaries and harbor lights; muffled the mountainside
But still, far, far below those lights pierced sky
And water: blue and violet, quick magenta flash
From welder's torch; and still the shoreline roared
Strumming the seas, drumming its rhythm hard
Beating out strong against the ocean's song:
The graveyard shift still hammering its way
Towards an unknown world, straddling new day.

1943.

67

Dorothy Livesay (1909-1996) was a writer of journalism, short fiction, autobiography and literary criticism. She was one of Canada's preeminent poets from late 1960's through the 1980's. Her work as a writer spanned seven decades, from her first publication, *Green Pitcher* (1928) through to the early 1990's when she was still a an active part of the Victoria literary community. From an early age she was encouraged by her mother, Florence Randal Livesay, journalist, poet and translator, and her father, J.F.B. Livesay, general manager of Canadian Press.

Livesay was educated at the University of Toronto and the Sorbonne. In the 1930's she became politically active in issues of social justice, a passion that continued throughout her life. Her works *Day and Night* (1944) and *Poems for People* (1947) were both recipients of the Governor General's Award for poetry. She taught in Northern Rhodesia in the late 1950's through the early 1960's and later served as writer-in-residence at universities across Canada.